Portrait of Your Ex Assembling Furniture

This book is dedicated to _____.

your ex's name

contents

new playlist

I was really looking forward to this
being a "Beyoncé's *Lemonade* on full blast"
kind of breakup

but it ended up being the
"same three Bon Iver songs on repeat" kind.

aftermath

I'm wonderful at ending things
before they begin

of picturing the details of our demise
all the way down to the clothing and

tchotchkes thrown
onto the street

the way they'll look sitting there
until you drive by to pick them up

broken
and wet from rain.

Sometimes it's me
piling them into my trunk

and sometimes
it hasn't rained

or it's only a sweatshirt
and pair of shoes

as opposed to everything
we've ever owned.

But it's always something.

One of us has to throw
something into the street.

Otherwise it wouldn't be considered a disaster.

Is ex-lover hyphenated?

I typed ex-lover into Google
and it told me I should sleep with you

that we'd have a shared intimacy
that makes for great sex without commitment.

I just wanted to know if I should hyphenate it.
It said either works:

ex-lover
or *ex lover*

Manic Pixie Dream Girl Sex Robot
4.9 Stars
Usually ships within 2-3 business days.
Want it tomorrow? Order within the next 2 hours.

Meet Manic Pixie Dream Girl Sex Robot, the number-one, best-selling sex robot from *Male Fantasy Inc.* Each Manic Pixie Dream Girl Sex Robot is unique and completely customizable. Choose her...

Name: Select from 12 distinctly fresh and unexpected names such as Willow, Piper, Joella or 10 more common, but still spunky names like Zoe.

Hair color: Whether you're looking for a classic brunette, a spunky red head, or a girl growing a full-on rainbow out of her head, *Male Fantasy Inc.* has you covered. Select from 20 different hair colors, including our limited edition Spontaneous Adventure Blue. (Note: All Manic Pixie Dream Girl Sex Robots come with bangs.)

Eye color: Manic Pixie Dream Girl Sex Robots can accommodate up to two different eye colors, including dark brown, light brown, dark blue, light blue, and green. Bored of light blue? Simply remove the plastic eyes from their sockets, flip them over and reveal her secondary eye color.

Tattoos: Choose from a booklet of 250 unique color and black and white designs, with varying levels of visibility, ranging from "clearly visible in public" to "completely hidden from all parental figures."

Each Manic Pixie Dream Girl Sex Robot comes equipped with her own bag of accessories, which are just as customizable as she is. Accessories include:

1 Unique and Easily Portable Musical Instrument (Options include: ukulele, recorder, or tambourine)

1 Band T-shirt (Options include: Joy Division, The Smiths, or Goo Goo Dolls)

1 Pair of Stylish Glasses (Note: She only needs them when reading.)

1 Used Book (Options include: The Catcher in the Rye, The Wind-Up Bird Chronicles, or The Collected Poems of e. e. cummings)

1 Pre-filled Spiral-bound Notebook (Filler options include: hand-written poems, song lyrics, or high-quality doodles)

1 Sentimental Item (Options include: a seashell from the beach she lost her virginity on in high school, a friendship bracelet from the girl she "experimented with" in college, or a blurry Polaroid of her dead cat)

What are you waiting for? Let Manic Pixie Dream Girl show you how magical and beautiful life truly is. Click "Get Started" and take the first step to meeting the #1 consumer-rated sex robot unlike any other.

Your Manic Pixie Dream Girl is ready to meet-cute you.

how to discuss your ex-lover

Speak of them in the past tense, like they are deceased, or moved to a far-off country devoid of an internet connection and cell reception.

Do not use their name in conversation, refer to them instead as "a friend of mine" or "someone I knew." This is less intimidating to present and future romantic prospects.

Allow them to take on the qualities of an estranged elementary school friend or a distant cousin whose name you occasionally forget. Always occasionally forget their name.

When someone mentions them, nod slowly, like you're trying to remember what their face looks like. Try to forget their face, especially if the person you're talking to has a face like their face.

If you find yourself in conversation with someone who regularly sees them, do not ask about them. Instead, talk about yourself, preferably using a lot of positive adjectives like *wonderful* and *amazing*, even if adjectives like *shitty* and *depressed* would be more accurate.

Rewrite memories as to make the new ones more accessible in conversation: Go to the museums you went to together, with someone new. Eat at the restaurants you ate at together, with someone new. Listen to the music you listened to together, with someone new. Speak about something new, with someone new.

Avoid discussing your ex-lover.

best-case scenario

I left the bar knowing
all you could report back was:
She got a nose ring and didn't ask about you.

I'm grocery store in love with you.

You're buying things I hate and I'm still in love with you. Like garlic hummus and a shit ton of canned beer.

You're wearing a denim jacket with a hand-sewn patch of my favorite band and your hair is that shoulder-length *I-woke-up-and-didn't-brush-it-but-it's-still-super-cute* kind of cute.

I'm imagining you sitting in your *cramped-but-in-a-cozy-way* apartment kitchen, with mismatched, flea market chairs and a big-ass hanging plant you haven't killed yet (because you're great with plants) and you're reading a beat-up paperback (probably Delta of Venus or something by Murakami) and not bothering to look up as I come in and pour a cup of some sort of exotic juice blend (like mango-peach or pineapple-I-don't-know, you're the one that bought it) and then I kiss you and I don't care that your breath smells like garlic because I'm in love with you.

I look up to see what color lipstick you're wearing in real life or if you're wearing any lipstick at all and realize in real life

you're gone

and I didn't ask for your number. I'm regretting every decision that brought me to checkstand #5, but also realizing you probably wouldn't go out with me anyways because I'm not wearing any makeup and I'm buying an off-brand, blue sports drink, a bottle of water, and a can of baby corn (which there is absolutely nothing sexy

about because it's not even eco-friendly and
what the fuck is baby corn anyways like is it
shrunken corn or corn that hasn't lived a full
life?)

Holy shit.

You're walking back to checkstand #5. You're
not wearing any lipstick and it looks great. The
supermarket clerk just unlocked the liquor case
and got you a really large bottle of Jack Daniels.

Holy shit. Please invite me to your party.

I'll pretend I like whiskey and make conversation
with your liberal arts friends in plaid shirts and
make out with you in your *cramped-but-in-a-
cozy-way* bathroom and knock over a bar of
lavender hand soap your hippie mother in
upstate New York made you and not care
because I'm in love with you.

Fuck, your receipt is printing.
The cashier is asking if I want to buy a bag.
(Fuck my life I left it in the car.) *Yes.*

I think about running after you, yelling something
romantic across the grocery store or giving you
my number on the back of a cereal coupon
with scribbled hearts but you're already too far
and I suddenly have to look at the floor

because I can't stand to watch you walk away
so quickly, in real life.

Automatic doors are the saddest kind of doors.
You can walk straight through
without even thinking about them.

l'amour du cinéma

You can only watch love stories
in black and white
in a foreign tongue

so when they say
I love you

you cannot recognize it.

Je t'aime
Te amo
Ti amo

Anything but
I love you.

Interstate 405

We met by accident

overflowing faucet
burnt dinner on stove
chipped paint
broken vase

I'm sorry.

I remember us
watching the flaming car on the highway
rubbernecking our love
in traffic set to sirens
we both thought:
That could have been us.

And in a way, it was.

Oh God, you're so beautiful
(or something like that)

I'm trying to remember what you said to me
when I took my shirt off.

Oh God, you're beautiful.
or *You're so beautiful.*

Yes, that.

The *so* made
so much of a difference.

I remember the first time you called me
Beautiful.
Actually, you said
nice.

You look nice.

The beautiful must have been in my head.
You say a lot of nice things in my head
(the things I want you to say).
You say *Oh God*
before a lot of them,
as if you have to combine shock
and ecstasy
and take the name of the Lord
all at once
because what you are trying to express
and who you are trying to express it to
is just that amazing.

Oh God, you're so beautiful.

I'm going to imagine you said that.

placeholder

I know we could never be *forever*
but maybe we can be *temporary*

and I think that would be enough right now.

alternate universe
in which you say "I love you"

- part one -

It is beautiful.

**alternate universe
in which you say "I love you"**

- part two -

It does not exist.

**a eulogy for my twin-sized mattress
with the flowers on it**

We stand here today on a sidewalk in
East Hollywood, surrounded by numerous
cigarette butts, an empty Taco Bell soda cup,
and half a dining room chair
to say goodbye.

Goodbye to a friend

who let my five year old, sugar-high self jump up
and down on her body

who magically blended my first period blood
into one of her pink rose petals

who looked away when I learned to touch myself

who didn't judge me when I did it again

who drove all the way to Los Angeles with me

who followed me up every flight of new
apartment stairs without complaint

who sometimes pretended to be a couch
to distract me from the fact I was too broke to
own an actual couch

who sang a squeaky chorus of springs
when I brought a boy home

who sang just as loudly when I brought a girl

who held me every night I was alone

who collected my tears, late night prayers,
dead skin cells, sleepless nights, restful nights,
every night.

Mattress, if you're listening, please know
the newfangled piece of foam I ordered off the
internet, the one that arrived in a box and
somehow expanded to mattress size,
will never hold a place in my heart like you did.

May you rest in bulky waste pickup peace,
knowing you lived a long, full life.

Amen.

K-town, 7:56pm

Shout out to
the 62-year-old Korean restaurant owner
who asked if I was your girlfriend.

I wasn't sure of the answer.
I'm glad that's cleared up now.

Hallelujah, I can buy my own goddamn flowers

Hallelujah
for the grocery store clerk
who handed me my $1.99 discounted flowers
like a gentleman
and said: *a gift for the lovely lady.*

Hallelujah
for the 24-hour drug store employee
putting up the 50% off sign
in the aisle with heart-shaped chocolate.

Hallelujah
for February 15th
and the fact that I have more than
ten dollars in my bank account
after my landlord cashed my rent check.

Hallelujah
for buying my own goddamn flowers
and looking at them with pride
as I unwrap hearts in my living room.

self-love

Anyone who says they've
never googled themselves

is lying.

revelation

You blame Catholic school
for your codependency issues.

Jesus was the original fuckboi.

the dangers of an all ages club

Welcome to your high school dream
long-haired boys with tight jeans
and misdemeanors
moshing
sweating
looking at you from afar
as they sell candy and cola
for what is probably their first job.

You avoid making eye contact with
the boy working the snack bar
because you know it's illegal
it has to be
he couldn't be any older than 17
stop
looking at him
with his long hair and sweet face
he's your high school dream
and you're 23
sober
and still thinking this way.

Run
fast, out of this place, past the bouncer
that is closer to your age, get outside
quick, before you commit an act of sin.
Stop
you arrive in the alley only to find
a row of pretty boys
chain smoking against chain link
blowing smoke from their perfect lips
hugging leather jackets to their skin.

Run faster
from this place in the dark
your legs are not long enough

to get there quick enough
they stop you and ask for a light
their cigarettes have gone out and
their eyes are alight as they
look you up and down
like something to capture
before curfew.

You keep a lighter in your purse for boys like this
that you want to kiss
no, you lie
you don't have a light.

And you escape the dangers of an all ages club
before it's even midnight.

pussy

I dreamt of you, again
last night

at my parents house we were
getting ready for a dinner party.

You came out of the bathroom
wearing a red lace top

(bare shoulders, your arms,
that smile).

Even in my dream I didn't have
the courage

to tell you
how beautiful you are.

Your eyes asked
How do I look?

I didn't look, didn't linger
as long as I wanted,

didn't want to give myself away.
Instead I walked quiet

into the bedroom past the bed
I wanted so badly

to kiss you on.
Searching

for something pretty enough
to wear for you.

in the dark

Driving past the rollercoasters at night
the metal curves
remind me of your body.

Shadowed, silent, looming
under moonlight and the hum
of highway incantations.

I've never wanted something inanimate
to hold me, so badly.
Please.

Most days, I am magic
turning everything into you
(disappearing acts in reverse).

Every thrift store, your shirt.
        Every parking lot, your car.
                Every movie theatre, your laugh.

It's easier at night
to miss you. You see
magic works better in the dark.

Sometimes I lay on my arm until it falls asleep
so I can hold on and
pretend it's yours.

Please.

You are a loud kind of lonely.

You are a loud kind of lonely.

You yell its name across the house,
tell it to go to bed at night,
feed it pancakes in the morning,
send it off to school,
throw it a birthday party,
keep a photo of it in your wallet
to show anyone who will look.

Look, you say. *Look at my lonely.*
Have you seen my lonely? How big it's gotten?
Do you remember when it was just a child?
When it couldn't speak? Couldn't walk?

Your lonely now knows how to run,
how to recite the alphabet,
how to hold its breath underwater
longer than you ever could.

At night you brush your lonely's hair,
tuck it into bed,
sing it a lullaby until it falls asleep,
then sit in the glow of its nightlight

wondering what to do with yourself
until it wakes up.

i am a quiet lonely

I am a quiet
lonely.

I never speak its name.

I am afraid to name something
I do not want to keep.

please google the word bisexual

Everyone's in the kitchen talking about
time machines.

Sam wants to travel back and win the lotto.
Emily says he can't pick that,
it's too cliché.
Sarah says we're speaking in hypotheticals,
so actually he can.

I'm standing in front of the fridge
grabbing a second beer
thinking about the time I thought my heart
was defective
because it would beat
against my ribcage
every time I saw a pretty girl.

I'm thinking about how
when I invited that cute girl from English over,
I shouldn't have sat frozen, at the opposite
end of the couch, the entire movie

when I asked Allison to junior prom
I shouldn't have added
"you know, as friends"

when the redhead at the art supply store
kept smiling at me and
I wrote my number on a parking garage stub,
I should have slid it across the counter to her

when I was smoking in the alley behind the bar
with the denim-jacketed bass player
I should have kissed her.

I'm thinking about how

when I googled the word *bisexual*
I realized maybe my heart
isn't defective after all.

I walk towards you.
I hand you a beer.
You collide your shoulder, your smile, into mine
and ask *What about you?*
What would you go back in time to tell yourself?

I look at
    your dirty blonde pixie
        strawberry cheeks
            chipped blue polish
                mismatched socks
and say

Nothing.

And by *nothing* I mean:

Otherwise I wouldn't be standing here
three kitchen tiles between us
talking about time machines
listening to my heart
beat loudly against my ribcage
thinking about how
I'm going
            to
                kiss
                        you.

unlearning straight

I'm dancing in circles right now
because there's nothing more frightening

than the thought of walking towards you
in a straight line.

I fucked it up this time
and all the times before

and all the times in the future because
I don't feel like myself anymore.

I don't think you'll ever see me not stumbling
over doorways and words.

Please know:
I'm not used to this clumsiness.

I'm usually on the other side
watching someone dancing in circles

wondering why they won't walk towards me
in a straight line.

we could be beautiful

We could be beautiful
if you knew what *we* was
and what beautiful ~~will~~ could be.

customer service isn't helping

There are instructions
for loving you

in size seven font
in six languages other than English

folded fourty-seven times
sealed in clamshell packaging

that's impossible to open without
slicing a finger off.

If you throw it against the wall
enough times

statistically one of the times
it will open.

Don't
wake the neighbors.

This is an emergency broadcast
a routine audit

a timed test.
Time starts

now.
Every clock in the room

is five minutes faster than the last.
Do you sometimes think about

what you'd remember
if you had amnesia?

Can you please find someone who knows
Mandarin? Or Cantonese?

Or one of the other five languages
these standardized test questions are written in?

I'm sorry
we are experiencing high call volumes.

I'm sorry
we are experiencing technical difficulties.

Please stand by.
Please allow 3-5 days to process your order.

Please press 0 to connect with the operator.
Press * for more options.

I love you.
Invalid entry.

portrait of your ex assembling furniture

We're adults now. We need a dining room table.
is actually Swedish for
Let's see if one of us is flammable.

The bearded employee
in the unfortunate yellow shirt
will tell you otherwise.
He'll tell you it's a great choice
a best seller
easy to assemble.
Do not believe anything you hear
with miniature meatballs and
strange berry juice in your system.
The high will wear off.

It takes approximately four minutes
for the novelty of driving with an oversized
cardboard box in your car to wear off.
Do not cry yet.
You haven't found out
you don't own a decent pair of scissors
or a hammer
or that there's only one beer left in the fridge.

Avoid making grunting noises while walking
backwards, up three flights of stairs.
You're not attractive when you do that.
Your living room is smaller than you think it is.
You know more curse words
than you think you do
they are just birthed by pieces of wood
falling on your foot.

You still don't know Swedish.

The bearded employee
in the unfortunate yellow shirt
could have told you this.
He could have also told you
there is a seven in one chance
of ending up with three leftover screws
and a piece of painted wood
(that looks incredibly important in a structural
sense but unnecessary in an aesthetic one).

Statistically speaking, a lot of couples
break up in furniture stores.
Remind yourself you made it out, together.
You made it to the parking lot, together.
You made it to the car, together.
You made it through the front door, together
somehow still in one piece.
You are beating the odds.

Remind yourself that the table
does not need to be functional.
You do not need to be functional.
Because after unpackaging everything
you will realize you never cook.

If you open up the little plastic tool bag
and rub the little wooden pegs together
fast enough
you will see sparks and distract yourself
from looking at the craigslist couch
you first made love on.
Do not sit on that couch while screwing anything
other than legs for the table whose name
sounds like a really great drug.

You want to get high on Ingatorp.
You need to get high on Ingatorp.

You're pretty sure the bearded employee
in the unfortunate yellow shirt
gets high on Ingatorp.

You black out.
You wake up on the couch, days later.
You don't know how many but pray
it's less than the return-policy 30.

You somehow get the box down
three flights of stairs, alone
into your trunk, alone
across the parking lot, alone
to the returns department, alone.

The bearded employee
in the unfortunate yellow shirt
will ask if anything was wrong with Ingatorp.

You will have to tell him:
that you are not an adult
that you do not need a dining room table
that you thought you could put each other
back together with a screwdriver
and Swedish instruction manual
that it turns out neither of you know Swedish
but both of you are flammable
and that Ingatorp is one fucking bad trip.

putain

I hear you yell fuck across the house
in French.

You tell me there's no translation for
how do you say it?

high school sweethearts
ah oui

high school sweethearts
that's what you are.

Putain
has become a melodic *I love you*

every argument in miniature,
a dollhouse disarrayed then

put back in place quickly
with ease.

I come home to the two of you arguing again
over whether or not to refrigerate the wine.

By the time I reach the kitchen
it's turned to laughter

bisous
kisses

Putain je t'aime.

hit and run

I was ready to drive across the 405
(in heavy traffic) to make out with you
but that night in the car I
leaned over to kiss you and
you were
        so
               far   away.

By the time our lips reached
I realized my mistake.

We crashed
into the second worst kiss of my life.
We swerved for a moment and then
pulled away.
I pretended like nothing happened,
like I didn't see this wreck coming
in slow motion
seconds before it happened,
like I could speed off into the night
without any damage,
like it didn't leave a massive scratch
the fender of my chest dented
inward.
Even in my dimly lit driveway
I could tell we were totaled.

I always drive too fast and
change lanes without a blinker.
But I've never crashed.
I promise I've never crashed
(at least not like this).

love reading

There's been so much effort
the psychic said.

I know
I wanted to say

but I was tired
so tired

I could only find the energy
to nod.

continental drift

I woke up to find myself
drifting
away from you
in pieces.

I cannot remember what we were like
whole
and you cannot fathom that we were
ever anything other than these parts.

It has happened over time
during the nights we were sleeping.

I woke up this morning and
found my arm couldn't reach you
asleep at the other end of the bed.

Darling, I think we're drifting.

We have to use maps now
to find ourselves in any place
together.

We have to factor in travel time
and traffic
and the cost of a bus ticket
if we don't want to drive.

And sometimes we have to board a ferry
on account of all the new seas.

I'm starting to forget we were ever called
Pangea, maybe it was something
we dreamed up late at night
a page in the obsolete geography book
buried somewhere

in a corner of our minds.

But it's the only way we can remember it:
a world of multiple seas,
too many coastlines to count.

you said to me (in the dark)

The fact that you are real
will never cease to amaze me.

I am hiding

from *I miss yous,*

from the want of waking
in the deepness of night
to find you
a body to hold onto
so I don't sink further,

from whispering our nightmares to each other
like kisses
like kissing ourselves
out of the dark.

Sometimes I wake up
in the deepness of night
to find lonely
a ghost I cannot hold onto,
I sink further.

There is no one left to whisper my nightmares to
so I am hiding under covers
whispering to myself
trying to kiss myself
out of the dark.

dancing alone

This is the sound of strangers
and songs we don't know

of grabbing on to the first body in the night
just to remember the taste

of a boy in the dark
drenched in sweat swaying next to you

feeling each others bones through clothes
kissing lips with no name

just so you can say
you know people in this city

who let you sample their soul.

welcoming the new girl

She talks about the men on the subway
like they're new
the unexpected, overnight kind of new
pimple on your forehead new
bloodstain in your underwear new
cowlicked bangs on picture day new
surprisingly inconvenient.

You can't remember a day without them,
without their winks when mother isn't looking
kissing noises from parked cars
sidewalk whistles
Let me get your number. Let me give you mine.

You want to tell her about the guy that grabbed
your ass in one tight squeeze and kept walking
didn't look back,
about the guy that groped you
in broad daylight at a gas station
while on the phone with his mother,
about the guy in the frozen food aisle
that asked to have sex with you
in the way people ask if it's going to be cold,
if they should bring a jacket.

She probably wouldn't believe you.

You watch her fingers find the pearls
around her neck. You want to ask her why she
wears them, tell her she looks like a fifties
housewife, but think maybe that was
the one thing in her mother's closet
she always wanted to wear.

She tells you about the men on the subway,
the ones that want to take her home

Can you believe it? she asks,
about the time she walked past the big prison
and the inmates made kissing sounds
from behind the bars of the 9th floor
What did they think was gonna happen?
she asks, about the teenage boy that yelled
fucking transvestite as he drove by her
Why would he yell that right near a school?

She tells you about the men she used to know
the ones that won't look her in the eye anymore
the ones that cross the street to avoid her.
It's like they're afraid of me, she says.
You watch her fingers reach for her coffee
realize it's empty.

What a wonderful thing, you say
to have men fear you.

She smiles.
I guess I didn't think of it that way.

You drop her off at the subway station,
watch her exit the car
walk long ballerina strides across the sidewalk
streetlight crown head held high in the night.

She moves with a dizzying grace
cuts edges around the night until she
disappears
leaves everything shattered
in a beautiful way.

You pick up a shard and see yourself,
realize she is everything you want to be.

a place once perfect was not a place at all

It ruins remembering,
going back
to a place that was once perfect
-ly large.

You have grown, or perhaps
this place has diminished in size,
either way something is [missing]
you don't know
if it's the space
or the people
or you—
one of them has lost its magic.

A place once perfect was not a place at all
but a time
you try to reach by reshaping ghosts
into a space that once seemed whole
-ly perfect.

the science of past tense

I imagined everything as it once was:

This table
a tree
each chair a branch.

This dress
a bundle of silkworms swimming
across my flesh.

This tea
leaves sprouting from my lips
with words
letters
falling
like scrabble tiles
onto this carpet that is now
three sheep in winter coats.

We are trapped

behind front steps
of uncarved mountains,
drowning in this sea of kitchen faucet drippings
releasing clouds
filling every room with rainstorms.

Every room
with you:
A pile of stardust
staring into all the elements
I once was.

There is a beauty in the past tense,
breaking everything down
into little pieces called

before.

We are all beautiful in the past tense,
so I am trying to imagine a world
in which we never discovered
the collection called *us.*

But as I am breaking it down
collapsing walls
unraveling sweaters into sheep
kitchen counters into dark caves
I am realizing:
I love every iteration of you
and me
because it can always exist as
us.

I now imagine everything as it once was:
stard*us*t.

anywhere but home

I found a place
where longhaired high school boys
go to smoke weed in their mothers' old Kias
kissed with Amoeba bumper stickers
and learners permit dings.

It's illuminated by the red neon glow
of the Supercuts sign
where $8 used to cut their dirty blonde hair
that now they grow
despite mothers wishes and fathers will.

I found it on a Friday after midnight
driving anywhere but home
twenty blocks from Thai Town and a twin bed
that's so old it creaks
whenever I turn
reminding me with every movement
that I'm moving alone
to this rusted lovers language
making out with ghosts.

This place feels like a graveyard
an island of asphalt stuck in a time
when whiskey was something to be stolen
from our father's liquor cabinet
and the perfect shade of lipstick could only
be found in our mother's makeup drawer
taken to attract the inexperienced lips
of some boy we were convinced
was our leather-jacketed soul mate.

Part of me wonders what will happen if I stay
parked next to two baby-faced blondes
trading cigarette smoke

and occasional words.

I watch the rhythm of their hands
lift lighters to the paper between their lips
until one looks my way and our eyes meet.
His clean blue and my dirty brown mix
as we speak unspoken words
he doesn't understand
what a girl is doing alone in her car
on a Friday night
in the parking lot of a Supercuts
not smoking
just staring at the lights of the cars as they pass.

But I know we have a lot in common
his ghost and mine
and that five years from now he might return
to a parking lot like this
realize it's a graveyard of parked cars
and people
who don't want to go home.

silent drive

The trees speak five languages
(none of which you know).

The almond blossoms look like snow
false winter in California spring

65 on the highway you let your eyes blur
gloss the window

the petals
become snowflakes.

You position the air vent
to goosebump your wrists.

You want to change the radio station
but doubt there's anything better to listen to.

You're pretending too many seasons
haven't amplified the silence.

You've lost count of the times you
decided not to speak.

The trip takes seven hours.
You wonder how he fills them.

listen

I am learning to say *boy*.
I am learning to say *girl*.

I am learning how to tell you
they can both mean *lover*.

moonlight rollerway

The woman working the cash register at the
roller rink compliments the star stickers we
stuck on each other's faces, says we look
"shiny." I guess because "shiny"
is a word you use to describe new things
or old things that clean up nicely.
I'm not sure which one we are.

She's got a star tattoo on her ankle.
It's orange and green and mixed together
it looks a little like a rainbow.
At least, that's what she tells us.
I can't picture it.
But I don't tell her that because she looks ready
to lift up the hem of her acid-washed jeans
and put her foot on the counter to show us.
I start to get the sense this is the longest
conversation she's had all night.

You tell her about the tattoo you want to get
above your shoulder blade.
You contort your neck to look at the spot
as if it's already there.
The woman stands up off her chair to look
as if it's already there.
She sits back down and nods.
"Oh yeah" she says, "you definitely should."

You smile.
Your teeth look whiter than I remember.

She tells you about how she wants to take her
mom to the tattoo parlor for her birthday
and get little matching hearts on the back of their
necks.

You tell her that'd be cute.

I'm not sure what to say
because I'm afraid of needles
and commitment.

I watch the couple walking over from the
parking lot and notice the way their arms are
entwined at the elbow and wonder how they're
able to hold hands like that.

It looks difficult
or comfortable
I'm not sure which one.

They're wearing white t-shirts
and the girl has on white denim shorts and white
sneakers and the overhead lights make them
look like a walking piece of moonlight.

The woman spots them and looks a little sad.
I'm not sure if that's on account of them being
entwined so complexly and comfortably
or because she has to stop talking about
what color her heart should be
(neon pink or yellow).

You tell her to have a good night
and she presses the buzzer to let us in.
I hold the door open for you.
You stop and look back at the ticket booth.
"I feel bad" you say.
I ask why.
"I feel like we're supposed to invite her to come
with us."

As we lace up our skates I think about how

she's going to spend all night behind a glass
window watching moonlight after moonlight pass
her by.

I look out onto the rink and see all the people
gliding in circles, bathed in disco-light kisses.

You fall into orbit
effortlessly.
"Come on", you yell.

I try to find the courage to let go of the wall.
I try to remind myself we're "shiny"
or at least, that's what she told us.
But I start to wonder if that's just what
everyone else looks like from behind the glass.

I hug the edge of the ring and start to move.
I focus all my energy on not falling.
I make it around once and then grab back
onto the edge.

I try to find you in the sea of fast-moving bodies
but I can't.
I'm just holding on
watching moonlight after moonlight pass me by.

bisous

We kiss all our friends
once on each cheek
not close enough
for the lip-gloss to stick.

I pretend I don't dream of losing
all my lip-gloss on your skin.

richter scale

Tell me
on a scale of 1 to disaster
how beautiful we are.

I promise I'll reinforce every shelf in our house
so that nothing breaks when we lie to each other
and say:

everything is fine
everything will work out
everything we hate will fall
between the cracks of the San Andreas.

We could be a perfect ten
if we shook everything in sight
out of sight
and screwed everything near the wall
into the wall

so that when the floors cave in
at least our vases will be intact
and our flowers can die

in a beautiful still life.

men like me

I like men with flaws, she said
big gaping holes, deep scars, chipped edges
I like them rough.

Because only men who have wrestled with
demons and tattooed lovers to their skin
know what beauty is.

I like men who fall
onto pavement and into bad situations.
I like to see the bruises on their knees.

Because only men who are used to
hitting the ground hard
can fall for someone like me.

I like men who run fast
wild and fearless in this city of noise
seeking silence and someone to hold.

Because only two sailors
who have been through a storm can
see the beauty in a pile of weed-covered dirt.

I've been through so many storms
I no longer see weeds, only something tall,
strong, making its way through the dirt

just like me.

I'm trying to get a poem out of you.

Isn't this what they do in the movies?

This downtown rooftop, stolen wine, everyone's
gone home and you've got the building keys
kind of kissing.

When you open the door I realize I only want to
kiss the photograph version of you (but the taxi
left, and I'm lonely).

I wonder how long I can go without kissing you,
if I can go without kissing you.

I realize the answer is *no*
when you find a way to clumsily stumble
your lips onto mine.

*Did you spend your entire life watching movie
kisses? Think, hey that looks really easy, but not
practice until right now?*

You tell me how great of a kisser I am.
I say *thank you* because I don't know how to
phrase *You're the worst kisser ever* in a more
polite way.

Now that I've kissed you, I decide I can leave.

Now that you've kissed me, you decide to take
me downstairs, cue up a song you've clearly
dreamed of making out to, ask me if I know the
artist, look a little disappointed when I reply
correctly with the name of the twenty-something
Canadian whose fan base includes a lot of boys
who wear Supreme hats.

Are you trying to make this an indie movie?

You kiss me again.
I can tell you're having a great time.
I'm not having a great time.

You offer to give me a ride home.
I pretend to like your convertible with racing
stripes on it. I say *Nice car* because I don't know
how to phrase *This is the douchiest car ever* in a
more polite way.

You cue up your I'm-going-eighty-on-the-
highway-with-a-girl-I-just-kissed music
which sounds a lot like the *Drive* soundtrack
with some EDM mixed in.

You roll down the windows so you can watch my
lose hair dance in the wind. You run your hand
along my stockings as I stare out at the city
and prepare to avoid awkward, unwanted eye
contact once we hit a stoplight and you rev your
engine for added effect.

We finally make it to my house and as you kiss
me goodnight I think about how much
mouthwash I can feasibly swallow without dying.

I step out of the car and you rev the engine one
more time for good measure before speeding off
into the night.

I realize you're probably trying to get a movie out
of me. And I'm trying to get a poem out of you.
So I guess it all evens out in

The End.

your lumber sexual soul mate has a girlfriend

It's not you, it's the universe
telling you you're screwed
and not being screwed
by the attractive, bearded hipster
in skinny jeans and a plaid shirt
standing in front of you in vintage boots
(he doesn't have to buy used shoes but he does,
he chooses to buy boots once worn by another
man, and wear them...better).

He is tall
he is handsome
he is the reason lumber sexual is a thing.
He is your soul mate and he keeps smiling at
you
and you keep smiling back
and he keeps talking to you
and you keep talking back
and he must be a compatible astrological sign
because this is going very well

until something in the cosmos finishes cutting
straight through you, straight through all the
tree rings you've built with this man
over many, many minutes
and you hear the sound of hope uprooting itself
as you fall
alone
in this fucking metaphorical forest
of single people.

He left it a while ago.
He's just here to cut down trees and leave.

departures

You drove me to the airport
in rush-hour traffic

and I'm trying to decide if that means
you love me

or at least want to entertain the idea
of loving me.

As I walk through airport security
with my shoes off

I entertain the idea
of someone loving me

(of you loving me).
I decide I like it.

I realize
I'm flying away from it.

the future

I visited the future last night.

You had computers in your eyes
and metal plates
drilled into your heart.

When I woke up
I realized I wanted you
back
as a robot
or as a man,
it doesn't matter which one.

I just want you there
waiting for me

in the future.

**postcard from an alternate universe
in which we're together**

Wish you were here.

leftovers

We saran-wrapped decisions,
left them in the fridge to be

forgotten
until we smelled the rot

realized we wasted
a perfectly good Friday night

waiting for you
to text back.

I threw it out

promised we'd never do it again
promised we'd eat it whole next time

in one bite save nothing
for later

because there is never a later
that tastes as good as right now.

Tonight, we will sleep with our bellies
brimming with right now.

how far to swim

Someone said you will miss it less
as you get further away.

Wave and wave and wave
until your hand is larger than it
until it drowns
under the horizon of your palm
and disappears.

You count the seconds
and watch the water speed below you
wave by wave by wave
and think about how much further
you'll have to swim
to reach it.

This many
then this many
then this many.

You lose count.
You see the next shore.
You realize
you were in love

with closeness.

bring down the house

Imagine you know how to dance.

Now dance
with tears in your eyes.

We do not have enough room for sadness.

Ballet, swing dance, fox trot, break dance
break every rule: line dance in a circle, two step
with one foot in the grave.

Let's all get in a drum circle
and listen to our heartbeats.

Bring down the house so there's nothing left
but disco ball shards and the memory
of feeling alive
of moving in a way that doesn't leave any bones
excluded from the party.

Everyone's invited. Especially you.

Leave your wristwatch at the door.
Leave your shoes at the door.

Soon there will be nothing left
but the dance floor

and you.

about the author

Born in the fog of San Francisco, Nicolette Daskalakis is an award-winning writer, filmmaker, and internationally-exhibited photographer. She is the author of "because you're now banging a French girl" and "All The Boys I Never Kissed". She is based in Los Angeles, where she spends most of her time listening to 60s French pop while stuck in traffic.

www.nicolettedaskalakis.com